CONVERSATIONS WITH LONDONERS

UK Olympics 2012:
Gateway to a Parallel Reality

By Chandra Bouri
Second Edition

The moral right of Chandra Bouri
to be identified as the author of this work has been asserted.
All photos of the Stratford Area have been taken by the author.

ISBN: 978-0-9562192-4-4

<u>ACKNOWLEDGEMENTS</u>

I am grateful for the support and help I received from the unseen helpers during the preparation of this book.
Furthermore, this book would not have been possible without the unselfish support of my wife, Kay.
I am grateful to Eesha for acting as one of the proof readers for this book.
I am also grateful to Amninder for driving me to Stratford to enable me to take some of the photos used in this book.
Chandra Bouri

18th July 2012

About the Author

Chandra Bouri, was born in Nairobi, Kenya in September 1951. He settled in London in 1968 and has been living in London for the past 44 years. His education, which began in Kenya was completed in East London.

His autobiography *Sunset on Mount Kenya* was published in 2005. His second book *2012: Leap into Time-Space* was published in April 2009. His third book *Seeking the Wisdom of the Lama* was published in June 2011.

A photo of the author is on the next page.

He can be contacted at the following email: chan@bouri.fsnet.co.uk.

CHANDRA BOURI

<u>Preface</u>

In the last week of June, I chose to fill in the Metropolitan Public Attitude Survey. Every year some 12,000 people are asked for their views. One question asked this time was whether I was worried about a terrorist attack at the forthcoming London Games. I didn't know what to answer so I asked my friends, neighbours and other Londoners what they thought .This is why this book came to be written.

Many Londoners are saying there are lots of creepy stuff surrounding these London Olympics. Take those triangular lights located on the main stadium - they are pyramid shaped. They don't like the one eyed mascots - reminds them of the All- seeing eye or the eye on the one dollar bill. It is claimed that the One Eye is a Illuminati Occult Symbol.

Londoners are saying there is too much occult symbolism surrounding the Olympic games and some of them call the games the Illuminati Games. They fear some kind of attack at the time of the opening ceremony or during the games or at the closing ceremony. Some even say the attack could come later this year.

It is stated the Olympics Logo actually means/spells ZION and the Illuminati Zionists are behind the London False Flag Operation. Hoping and praying that the UK can deliver safe Olympic games for all.

<u>July 18th 2012- London-UK</u>

<u>Contents</u>

CHAPTER ONE

Medals Table

I hope Team GB grabs 77 medals in total 30 gold, 17 silver and 30 bronze. After all we have the home advantage. We should be 3rd overall in terms of medals and in 4th position in the gold medal table.

My friends think that is a bit over optimistic and they reckon 60 medals in total. Gold being between 25 to 27, silver being between 15 to 20 and bronze being between 13 to 20.

CHAPTER TWO

Pointing the Finger

BA Advert Promotion

That was a strange advert I saw on TV the other week.
It was a BA advert which said don't fly during the Olympics .
Ok, so stay home and support Team GB.

Firstly it is strange for a national airline to say- Don't fly.
To me the very idea of showing a plane taxing along a public
road was very unusual - the first time I saw the advert I could
not believe my eyes. The memory of 9/11 is very fresh in my
mind although it happened a decade ago.

Secondly the lyrics seem to me to be badly chosen. The song is
"London Calling" by the Clash. In this song London Calling,
reference in made to the underworld, London is drowning, dec-
laration of war and battle coming down, the meltdown expect-
ed, the nuclear error, and so on. A bit strange to say the least.

The Prophecies of Benjamin Solari Parravicini

Parravicini drew scores of free flowing drawings and many of
these drawings have been identified as being drawings of future
events.

One such drawing done in 1972, which features a Torch and a
Bell amongst other things has been identified as being about the
London Stadium and also matches a place which is about two
kilometres from the Olympic Stadium in Hackney Marshes.

The bell, the torch, the Scythe of Death and the Arcelor-Mittal Tower Orbit figure are so easily recognisable in this drawing done by Benjamin Parravicini. How is it possible that Parravicini chose to draw the Olympic Stadium and the Hackney Marshes area decades ago and for what reason?

A bell was customarily rung at the time of William Shakespeare before his plays began. It has been announced that a giant tuned bell will be rung again at the London Olympics. This bell is the biggest in the world and weighs 27 tons.

The Arcelor-Mittal Orbit Tower has been specially designed for the Olympics.

The Rockefeller foundation

The Rockefeller foundation has postulated that 13,000 were killed in the 2012 Olympic bombing.[3] This from the document titled Scenarios for the future for the development of Technology and International Development. On its own it can be dismissed but taken together with predictive programming and the multitude of You-tube videos it makes one ponder if a message is being delivered.

____

[3]. See Page 34 of their 2010 report See www.rockefellerfoundation.org

CHAPTER THREE

You-tube videos referencing a False Flag Operation at the London Games

During the months of June and July many You-tube videos surfaced which state the possibility that a false flag operation will be carried out at the forthcoming London Games. Surely the police, MI 5, MI 6 and other governmental agencies must be aware of these videos.
There are several You-Tube videos which hint at or promote a False Flag Operation at the London 2012 games. How to sum up all the You-Tube videos which are there ?

I understand the following may happen after watching these videos:

1. The tube system may be targeted. Many videos hint at the London Tube Map. A bomb or several bombs in the tube network is a possibility.

2. Be very careful while using the Central Line out of Stratford going to the city. One of the videos hints or even states that the Central Line will contain the bombs. The Central Line runs directly under Hackney Marshes, Lee Valley and the Olympic Park.

3. There is reference to the earth physically moving. Perhaps part of the London underground collapsing in some sections of the network or made to collapse?

4. There are many references to Hackney Marshes and Lee Valley.

5. There are many references to Postal Code nine and Postal Code 10. I infer these could mean N9 or N10.

6. There are references to Clapton.

7. Big Ben may be targeted. In some videos you see a white van standing near Big Ben and later on another big white van blows up in the vicinity of Big Ben. In one of the Olympic adverts Big Ben gets knocked down an then all the world comes together as one world .Why knock down Big Ben? This does not make sense. The girl knocks it down with her foot.

8. A nuclear attack may be carried out.

9. There are references to Turnpike Lane.

10. There are references to - " Time bomb"- Kylie Minogue.

11. There are references to - "about to blow."
The last bit of Kesha Clip states - 'about to blow'.

12. The London Olympic Stadium can hold 80,000. The number 80,000 comes up in a video - and has been linked to the number of the total capacity at the stadium. The suggestion is that 80,000 people are in danger at the stadium.

13. Several videos hint that the strong possibility exits that the false flag operation will be carried out to advance the New World Order but that the religious extremists will get the blame.

14. A new power line tunnel has been built at Stratford Underground Station. This was suspended for more than 30 hours on 6th June 2012 due to flooding - speculation aired in the video - was this opportunity used to install explosives?

CHAPTER FOUR

Predictive Programming

The illuminati hides out in the open some of their agenda plans which they want to carry out. These propaganda media work as predictive programming.- letting the unsuspecting public 'know' a plan is in the offing to be carried out. One such plan- the London False Flag operation has been "announced" in many mainstream media productions e.g., in movies. music pieces, video games etc.

Post 9/11 it was found that there was many references to the destruction of the twin towers in New York. There was even a TV movie called *The Lone Gunmen* which aired on the 4th March of 2001 which depict a US plane on it way to the twin towers.

Similarly there are scores of You Tube Videos, cartoons and movies which mention negative themes round the London Summer Games of 2012.

Some are mentioned below:

Movies, books, plays, cartoons etc which make reference to the London Olympics

2008 TV Series "SPOOKS: CODE- 9"

This is a fictional nuclear disaster movie set at the London Olympics.

In 2010 an author called Tom Cain wrote a short story about a nuclear explosion at the Olympic Stadium and in Trafalgar Square. This was published in a UK paper.[2]

Others are as follows:

1. Cars 2. A 2011 movie. This is about secret agents - there are many countries which participate -the plot is about a bomb in London at a major event- this brings all the people together.

2. Anonymous. This movie refers to Stratford and Stratford Stadium. In this movie one of the themes is manipulation of the people - I.e. trying to make them revolt but they are betrayed and executed. 80,000 get killed.

3. V for Vendetta.

4. Operation Blackjack. A Telegraph slide show story. Although it is fictitious it is said to be predictive programming. Two white vans are seen on the Bridge.

5. The Dictator.

6. G.I. Joe 2.

7. Retaliation.

8. Reign of Fire.

9. 28 Weeks later.

10. Baal Storm God.

11. Harry Potter Half-Blood Prince.

12. Total Recall (2012).

13. The Iron Lady.

14. Splinter Cell Blacklist.

15. Mario & Sonic at the London 2012.

16. London 2012 (official video game).

17. 39 Steps (1978).

18. Hugo.

CHAPTER FIVE

Security Considerations

To police the games is going to be a big headache. Do you bring in a private force or use regular police? Or the army? Or All of them? In what proportion? The city needs to be kept safe. All the Olympic Venues need to be protected.

G4S was awarded the contract for nearly 300 million pounds to provide security at all the Olympic venues. They are a private security force which is responsible for security at the games. G4S employs nearly 700,000 men and women.

The MOD say they need to place surface to air missiles in six locations. One is the 17 storey Fred Wrigg Tower in Leyton-stone. Defence Minister Philip Hammond said the missiles are needed for national security. A small number of local residents in East London are concerned. The concerned residents of South London have banded together and do not want any mis-siles sited in their area.

13,500 troops will be deployed, including snipers and over 10,000 police. Also deployed will be carriers and sound can-nons. The Olympic Park will be guarded by sonic weapons. More that 50 teams of attack dogs will also be there. Also the Olympic Park has electrified fencing.

It was announced in Parliament on Thursday July 12th that a further 3,500 troops will be needed to provide security due to G4S's inability to supply enough guards in time for the games.

Lee Hazeldean- Whistle blower.

Undercover reporter Lee Hazeldean has managed to secure a job with G4S. Lee is an investigative TV reporter. He has made an interesting report about his findings.

Below are listed some of his claims.
.
 He has stated that plans have been made to evacuate the entire population of London. That is nearly 12 million people.

2. Since January 2012 American, UN and German troops have been passing through Woolwich barracks have now been housed along various locations across London. This evacuation may be needed in case of a biological or chemical event at the games.

3. He is concerned about lack of proper training. He said unemployed people have been signed up and their training has been rushed through. He says some recently trained employees cannot use the Hand Held Metal Detectors. This is a vital piece of equipment.

4. He said the Pedestrian Screened Areas have many below qualified team leaders.

5. He has revealed his findings at this time because he wants G4S to tighten its security.

6. He has said uniforms have gone missing.

7. He also fears that metal detectors will be switched off during busy times.

8. He does not believe the "Rapiscan" walk through machines being used at the games are very efficient. He says they are not sensitive enough.

9. There are 200,000 temporary coffins which have arrived in London from the USA. They can hold four people.

10. He says security training of officers needs to be increased.

It was reported in The Sun on Thursday July 12th that Al-Qaeda is plotting cyanide attacks at the games.[4]

According to the Telegraph article[5] only 4000 security staff out of the 13,700 needed have been found and G4S says it will now make a loss over the games of around £35 to £50 million It is becoming more evident that security has been mismanaged.

____

[4] Exclusive by Simon Hughes
[5] Telegraph 12th July 2012.

CHAPTER SIX

PHOTOS OF THE AREA ROUND THE OLYMPIC PARK IN STRATFORD

PHOTOS OF THE AREA ROUND THE OLYMPIC PARK IN STRATFORD

PHOTOS OF THE AREA ROUND THE OLYMPIC PARK IN STRATFORD

PHOTOS OF THE AREA ROUND THE OLYMPIC PARK IN STRATFORD

PHOTOS OF THE AREA ROUND THE OLYMPIC PARK IN STRATFORD

PHOTOS OF THE AREA ROUND THE OLYMPIC PARK IN STRATFORD

PHOTOS OF THE AREA ROUND THE OLYMPIC PARK IN STRATFORD

PHOTOS OF THE AREA ROUND THE OLYMPIC PARK IN STRATFORD

PHOTOS OF THE AREA ROUND THE OLYMPIC PARK IN STRATFORD

PHOTOS OF THE AREA ROUND THE OLYMPIC PARK IN STRATFORD

PHOTOS OF THE AREA ROUND THE OLYMPIC PARK IN STRATFORD

PHOTOS OF THE AREA ROUND THE OLYMPIC PARK IN STRATFORD

PHOTOS OF THE AREA ROUND THE OLYMPIC PARK IN STRATFORD

PHOTOS OF THE AREA ROUND THE OLYMPIC PARK IN STRATFORD

CHAPTER SEVEN

Conspiracy Theories

Time after time it has been stated that the NWO wants to implement its plans. It may be that they plan to use the London Olympics to plan an act of terrorism to implement their Agenda.

There is also a lot of talk of a Illuminati Disasters card showing a fallen tower and people in Olympic clothing. Is that meant to convey a message that something is being planned to happen at the London Olympics?

UNDERCOVER ALIEN

See Undercover Alien's numerous You-tube videos and you will be amazed. I was. They contain much useful information. Only accept what resonates with you and discard the rest.

Rik Clay

Since the Olympics were awarded to London in 2005 Rik Clay had been looking at the symbolism of the games. He reckoned that the area in East London was left as wasteland for all those years so that it could be available for the games in the future. He had also pointed out that the Olympic Torch symbolises the Moon Goddess Isis.

According to Rik Clay there will be a planned "alien visitation" alongside the anointment of an "end times messiah". He believes there will a significant event connected to the 2012 Olympic Games and that the 2012 logo spells Zion. Rik Clay has been credited with spotting that the 2012 logo spelled Zion although some credit Ian Crane for this finding.

<u>Higher Self Theory</u>

Many people believe that this cycle is coming to an end. They have seen in the past few years that earth changes have really increased - increased floods, earthquakes and volatile seasons. They accept that new energies are coming to this earth.

If at this time - now or at the Winter Solstice Alignment of December 21st or even after - if their work in this incarnation has finished they realize on the soul level they are ready to pass on to the spirit life although in the physical waking life they do not do know this. It may be that either they have learnt the lessons earmarked for this life or fulfilled their purpose for being on the Earth at this time in history.

So from a higher self perspective they are ready to leave although they know it not on the physical plane. So if a group of people who have finished with this life may find themselves travelling together in the same plane, bus or car in which may result in their death. They would not know physically when awake this knowledge that they are meant to go to the spirit life. So they may visit the same venue, or the same location. If there is a stampede or some other reason in a public place maybe their higher self chose to go to the spirit life in that manner. It is reputed that as we come to the so called end of an age (Mayan Calendar) of the 7 billion people on the planet there may be some who know on a higher lever that the have finished with this life and if there is a group of people who are meant to go to the spirit life together in a public place they will unconsciously come together to the same place.

God forbid anything happens at the forthcoming Olympics.

CHAPTER EIGHT

PHOTOS OF THE AREA ROUND THE OLYMPIC PARK IN STRATFORD

PHOTOS OF THE AREA ROUND THE OLYMPIC PARK IN STRATFORD

PHOTOS OF THE AREA ROUND THE OLYMPIC PARK IN STRATFORD

PHOTOS OF THE AREA ROUND THE OLYMPIC PARK IN STRATFORD

PHOTOS OF THE AREA ROUND THE OLYMPIC PARK IN STRATFORD

PHOTOS OF THE AREA ROUND THE OLYMPIC PARK IN STRATFORD

PHOTOS OF THE AREA ROUND THE OLYMPIC PARK IN STRATFORD

PHOTOS OF THE AREA ROUND THE OLYMPIC PARK IN STRATFORD

PHOTOS OF THE AREA ROUND THE OLYMPIC PARK IN STRATFORD

PHOTOS OF THE AREA ROUND THE OLYMPIC PARK IN STRATFORD

PHOTOS OF THE AREA ROUND THE OLYMPIC PARK IN STRATFORD

PHOTOS OF THE AREA ROUND THE OLYMPIC PARK IN STRATFORD

PHOTOS OF THE AREA ROUND THE OLYMPIC PARK IN STRATFORD

PHOTOS OF THE AREA ROUND THE OLYMPIC PARK IN STRATFORD

PHOTOS OF THE AREA ROUND THE OLYMPIC PARK IN STRATFORD

PHOTOS OF THE AREA ROUND THE OLYMPIC PARK IN STRATFORD

PHOTOS OF THE AREA ROUND THE OLYMPIC PARK IN STRATFORD

PHOTOS OF THE AREA ROUND THE OLYMPIC PARK IN STRATFORD

CHAPTER NINE

The Opening Ceremony

The Opening Ceremony could easily surpass the one held in China in 2008. It has been claimed that the Opening Ceremony is in reality a major satanic ceremony with altars, statues, wands, Masonic symbols and a Mosh Pit. People say it is nothing like a Christian Ceremony.

There is at least a hundred videos which keep hinting that the Olympic Games are some a kind of watershed event. Expect an event to happen which will shake the UK and Europe. The dates range from 27th July to 12th August. Many of these videos hint at a nuclear explosion at the stadium.

The general theme appears to suggest a bomb on the underground, or attempted explosions at the Olympic Park . What is supposedly a fun and happy occasion is not reflected in the choice of music and lyrics. Lyrics suggest revolution, rebellion and destruction.

Many Occultists I have talked to in London suggest that the themes chosen to be represented in the Opening and Closing ceremonies have an occult hidden agenda behind them.

Tree on top of St Michael's Tower at the Tor

I understand the Tor features in the Rural England scene with a tree on the top of the Tower at the Tor at the Opening Ceremony.
People say this is strikingly like a scene from the movie Watchers. So we have the Watchers theme repeated several times. Theme about the Giants of Old is also part of the Olympics. Are they trying to send a signal for the Nephilim to return?

CHAPTER TEN

Tolling the Ancient Bell

It is claimed that the Olympics honour both Zeus and Pelops. And the ritual sacrifices are performed in honour of them alongside the sports ceremonies. Many people state that the tuned bell is an acoustic devise which rings in another dimension. So whose attention are they trying to attract? A ritual ceremony, no doubt. Are they trying to connect or reach or attract or awaken some being in another dimension by the use of ritualistic paraphernalia? Are they trying to send energy to the giants of old? Are they trying to evoke supernatural forces? Are they trying to change the global time line? Do they want to do away with established authority here - the present status quo? Do they want to change the prevailing Agenda?

The Orbit Tower is a strange structure, maybe it has uses beyond the ones which have been stated. The triangular shaped Shard only opened in July. And now we have the Orbit Tower. Two strange structures. And a tuned Bell.

The Medals

Some people have said that they have found occult symbols on them such as portals.

CHAPTER ELEVEN

The Closing Ceremony

Right at the very end the ceremony will be handed to
Rio De Janeiro for 2016. Would be good to watch the Rio pres-
entation at the closing ceremony. I understand possibly the
1971 David Bowie hit , Life on Mars? may be performed at the
closing ceremony.

CHAPTER TWELVE
The Illuminati Symbols

Watch out for the symbols of the One Eye, the Owl and the Pyramids.

The All-Seeing Eye

The "All-Seeing Eye" could be regarded as the eye of God or the eye of Satan or Lucifer or Horus. If you watch the opening and closing ceremonies see how many examples of "the one eye" you can spot.

Wenlock and Mandeville- The Mascots

People say they are sinister and scary - some call them "Illuminati monsters." Each one of the black eyes is actually a camera. Some say the words Wenlock and Mandeville actually translates as "We unlock the devil in man." However there are also other explanations of what the words mean. This black eye seems to have been crowned with a capstone.

Owl and Pussycat Opera

During the Olympics at some stage an owl is to sail down the canals in East London! Would be a sight to see!

Pyramids and Capstones

It is clear the triangular design of the lights look like a pyramid. Keep a lookout for more pyramid shapes during the opening and closing ceremonies. The pyramid base without a capstone would mean something which is symbolised by the pyramid has not yet completed and it is hoped will complete some day.

CHAPTER THIRTEEN

What people are saying

Either just before the start of the Olympics, during it or just after the games end watch all political and natural events. Whether Russia moves into Syria to protect its ally or President Obama makes a peace agreement with Iran, or whether tensions in the Korean Peninsula explodes into exchange of hostilities - it is anyone's guess but it will certainly be worth watching world events at this time. I heard on the news on Thursday July 12th that even Israel has stated if the situation in Syria gets worse and the chemical weapons stockpiled by Syria are in danger of falling into other hands they will go in to Syria. They say they want to make sure that chemical weapons don't fall into the wrong hands.

Some people have said Prince Philip is very ill and may succumb to his illness in the next few months. Surely a rumour - nothing in the press about this. So watch the royals and pray all is well with them.

Some people reckon World War 3 will be triggered to bring the Satanic New Age, Oneness, New World Order - this has been symbolised by the rainbow at different places including the Illuminati Denver Airport Paintings. Some people want to bring about a Satanic New Era and in the process knock out 90 percent of the world's population.

Some people reckon there is a satanic, illuminati, Zionist plan in the offing for the dark forces to establish London as the capital of the New World Order. They say the hymn New Jerusalem (which so resonates with me) about the sword not sleeping and one making mental efforts to build Jerusalem in England's Green and Pleasant Land is not what I think it is. Something to think about.

Other things which people comment on are below:

Why is Julia Gillard, Australian PM not attending?

Why is Shimon Peres not attending?

The London 'Scirpmylo Festival'" covers the whole period of the Olympics (27 July - 12 August) in Hackney. People are saying why reverse the word Olympics - for what reason? Strange. It is said that Scirpmylo is Olympics backwards - meaning it is satanic symbolism - apparently significant.

Traffic in East London will come to a standstill on most event days.

People are saying the one-eyed mascot design and the 2012 logo was forced through despite objections.

People are saying it looks like the cost of policing and securing the games will exceed the cost of hosting them.

People are saying that the only reason they can think the roof top missiles will be needed is to stop an airliner or a flying vehicle heading for the Olympic park or the Olympic venues.

People are saying they don't have to fly a hijacked aircraft into the Olympic Stadium but into any of the tall buildings in the city. That will stop the Olympics. People generally agree that if terrorists cannot get to the Olympic Stadium they will choose an easier target or the one not so well protected. Some are saying they would not need to crash a plane but get into the no-fly zone and the rooftop missiles would do the rest bringing down the plane on to the populace. A no-fly zone has gone into effect from Friday morning July 13th. All commercial air space round southern England is in the hands of the military and is run out of RAF Northolt.

People are beginning to question whether security was deliberately messed up and the shortfall of the guards not reported in good time.

People are saying that any Olympic venue could be targeted even as far from London as Brands Hatch, Weymouth or Old Trafford.

People are saying like in the 1984 LA Olympic games - at the closing ceremony people dressed as spacemen will put in an appearance.

SUMMARY OF WHAT PEOPLE HAVE TOLD ME

Adding all the signs together indicates that something is afoot.

So we have the logo which spells Zion.

Also there is a Illuminati Card Game of disasters - one card of which shows people wearing the Olympic colours and a fallen tower. This tower has a likeness of Big Ben. Then we have the one-eyed Mascots, Pyramid shaped lights and occult opening and closing ceremonies. In addition we have songs which are being used to advertise this event which do not feel right. Many of these songs speak of war and destruction. This is a big spectacle of sports, right? Then there is a Festival which has been named Scirpmylo - reversing the word Olympics which runs during the duration of the Olympics. Also people claim that the start of the Olympics coincides with the Jewish day of mourning i.e., 9th of Av.

We even have President Obama's statement to one of his aides that Israel will attack Iran if the "Olympic Games" fail. Of course in this context "Olympic Games" refer to the Cyber Attack Programme which is being waged against Iran's computers to do with their Nuclear Program. Strange that this bit of information is currently in the news at this time as the Olympic games are coming up.

CHAPTER FOURTEEN

So what is likely to happen?

Hopefully nothing bad will happen. Most likely nothing will happen. London will deliver a safe Olympics for all. However many people have said they are getting out of London for the duration. But anything can happen. A planned or staged event could happen. There may be groups out there which may even want to disrupt the reporting of the Olympics.

The stadium has been built on a toxic radioactive dump. Even a small non-nuclear explosion could bring the radioactivity to the top. The Olympics may have to be cut short. Maybe the Paralympics may not be held.

When the capstone is attached to the pyramid

It is understood that the capstone will be attached to a pyramid and lighted up at the Olympics. Attaching it to the pyramid will cause it to light up. People say this symbolises the celebration of the victory of the one world government. Others says it is celebrating the achievement of Lucifer's ascension.

It has been reported that respected UFO researcher Nick Pope says to watch the skies for the aliens during the Olympics. There are many other people who believe that at the closing ceremony the New World Order will stage a mock UFO invasion. They say August 12th 2012 is the day when contact will be made. Henceforth the history of the world will change. My personal belief is that the real ETs are already known to the governments of the world so it makes me wonder, which group of aliens is supposedly making contact in this manner?

As this book goes to print there is no let up with regard to You-tube videos. The theme of sacrifice is very strong. Also the theme of sudden violent change is very strong. A new virus, shortage of some foods and magnetic changes on the earth is hinted at during the remainder of this year.

Somehow it is claimed that these Olympics will usher in a time-line which is vastly different from the one we live in. A new Pope, Queen abdicating her crown in favour of Charles or even William. Perhaps after 60 years on the throne she thinks she has fulfilled her duty to her people and her nation.

Gradual change always works out in the long term. YET it is quite clear some people want to manifest a time line where they want wars, anarchy and chaos to rule the day.

BIBLIOGRAPHY

To research this book I was on a time limit of about two weeks. I just typed into Google phrases such as Olympics Security, Olympics and conspiracies, Olympics and dreams etc. Then I narrowed them down by adding London.

I also talked to friends and neighbours. I also chatted to people and officials at the Westfield shopping centre at Stratford also looked at conspiracy sites on the net. To name a few, Red Ice Creations, Godlike Productions and Above Top Secret. Many alternate media sites were consulted.

I consulted numerous You-tube videos - just typed 'London Olympics' in to the search engine and scores of sites come up. This book would not have been possible without the help of You-tube videos by Undercover Alien, Rik Clay and scores of others. The Open Scroll Blog has proved very useful too.